101
School Cafeteria
Jokes

by Jovial Bob Stine

illustrated by Don Orehek

SCHOLASTIC INC.
New York Toronto London Auckland Sydney

ISBN 0-590-43759-3

36 35 34 33 32   6 7 8/0

Printed in the U.S.A.   01

First Scholastic printing, August 1990

DON'T LOSE YOUR LUNCH OVER THESE LUNCHTIME GAGS!

Mary: What's sticky, purple, has 16 legs, and is covered with thick, brown hair?

Larry: I don't know. What?

Mary: I don't know, either. But they're serving it today in the cafeteria.

Sam: Every day I get the same boring thing for lunch! I'm sick of a peanut butter sandwich and an apple, day after day.

Pam: Well, why don't you ask your mom to give you something else?

Sam: I can't. I pack my own lunch!

George: Do you eat with your left hand or your right hand?
Della: My right hand.
George: That's weird. I always use a fork!

Q: What do you call a kid named Charles who eats three helpings of cafeteria lasagna?

A: Upchuck.

Morty: This beef stew tastes just like dog food!

Cook: Don't be ridiculous! How can cat food taste like dog food?

Sharon: Why do you eat everything with your knife?

Mort: My fork leaks!

Cafeteria Worker: What would you like for lunch?

Harry: Make it a surprise.

Cafeteria Worker: All right. BOO!!

Mort: Last week they served a special chicken in the school cafeteria, and everyone was tickled.

Mary: Why's that?

Mort: They forgot to remove the feathers!

Bill: Why are you eating that brown sack?

Jill: My mom packed me a bag lunch.

Fred: Hey, there's a long, black hair in my macaroni!

Cook: It can't be mine. I put my hair in the vegetable soup today!

Sam: Is it good manners to eat chicken with your fingers?

Pam: No. You should eat your fingers separately!

Mary: One good thing about this lunchroom is that we can eat dirt cheap.

Larry: But who wants to eat dirt?!

Mike: These eggs are funny-looking.

Mark: I don't get the yolk!

Mary: Look, there are forks, knives, spoons, and hammers today. What are the hammers for?

Larry: I guess they're serving pound cake!

Sharon: Why won't you sit with Tommy?

Mary: He has such a big mouth, he can sing a duet with himself!

Sharon: Oh, come on. His mouth isn't that big.

Mary: Oh no? Look at him. Did you ever see anyone else eat a banana sideways!

Sam: Should you eat this cafeteria food on an empty stomach?

Pam: No. You should use a plate.

Pam: Is it okay to eat hot dogs with hands?

Sam: No. Hot dogs don't have hands!

Bill: What do caterpillars taste like?
Sharon: How should I know?
Bill: You just ate two of them in your salad!

Sam: What's this in my soup?
Cafeteria Worker: How should I know? I can't tell one bug from another!

Mary: Is this steak or liver?
Cafeteria Worker: Can't you tell by the taste?
Mary: No.
Cafeteria Worker: Then what difference does it make?

Debbie: Why are you eating those cookies so fast?

Larry: I want to eat as many as I can before I lose my appetite!

Sam: What's brown and can see just as well from either end?

Sharon: I don't know. What?

Sam: A horse with its eyes shut!

Sharon: Very funny. But what's that got to do with school cafeterias?

Sam: What do you think that hamburger on your plate is made of?

First Lunchroom Worker: I told you to put salt in the salt shakers. What's taking you so long?

Second Worker: It's hard to get the salt through the little holes!

MONSTERS IN
THE SCHOOL CAFETERIA

Two monsters from outer space landed on earth and invaded a school cafeteria. They looked around, then went over to the garbage cans, which were filled to the brim.

The two monsters lifted the garbage cans to their enormous mouths and began to chew loudly. After they had eaten everything, one monster turned to the other and said, "What do you think?"

"Well," said the second monster, "the crust is good, but the filling is a bit rich!"

A big monster and a little monster from outer space landed on earth and ended up in a school cafeteria. The little monster saw the cook and began chasing him around the kitchen. But when he caught the cook, he tickled him under the arm and then let him go.

The terrified cook ran away, with the little monster chasing right behind him. Once again the monster caught the cook and tickled him, then let him go.

"Hey, Junior," the big monster said angrily, "how many times do I have to tell you not to play with your food?!"

Two giant fish creatures from outer space landed on earth and ended up in a school cafeteria. They immediately dived onto the cafeteria workers and gobbled them up.

When they were finished, one fish creature turned to the other and said, "That's the problem with humans. They taste good, but there are too many bones!"

DON'T KNOCK THESE LUNCHTIME KNOCK-KNOCKS!

Knock, knock.
Who's there?
Noah.
Noah who?
Noah better place to eat than this
   cafeteria?

Knock, knock.
Who's there?
Frank.
Frank who?
Frank you very much for eating my
   lunch for me!

Knock, knock.
Who's there?
Evan.
Evan who?
Evan elp us if we swallow this food!

Knock, knock.
Who's there?
Henny.
Henny who?
Hennybody got a stomach pump?

Knock, knock.
Who's there?
Fred.
Fred who?
Fred chicken never used to be green
    before — did it?!

Knock, knock.
Who's there?
Sarah.
Sarah who?
Sarah way to digest this food?

Knock, knock.
Who's there?
Moira.
Moira who?
Moira you eat, the sicker you get!

Knock, knock.
Who's there?
Barry.
Barry who?
Barry sorry I ate that mystery meat
   special!

Knock, knock.
Who's there?
Juan.
Juan who?
Juan more bite. Then I'm leaving!

Knock, knock.
Who's there?
Sandy.
Sandy who?
Sandy doctor — quick!!

MORE LUNCH LINE
PUNCH LINES!

Sam: Why are you rubbing your food on the back of your shirtsleeve?
Pam: They said it was elbow macaroni.

Mary: Look, there are forks, knives, spoons, and crowbars today. What are the crowbars for?
Larry: That's for getting the crust off the chocolate pudding!

Q: What's green and fuzzy and sits in a bun?

A: The hamburger they serve in the cafeteria.

Q: What's green and fuzzy and sits in a chair?

A: A kid who's just eaten the hamburger in the cafeteria!

Morty: Hey — there's a fly in my macaroni!

Cook: Ssshhh. Not so loud, or everyone will want one!

Margie: Mmmmm. The tomato soup looks delicious today.

Cook: It's not tomato soup. I cut my finger.

Sarah: Let me guess what you had for lunch. Spaghetti, meatballs, beets, and mashed potatoes.

Sam: That's amazing. Did you read my mind?

Sarah: No. Your chin!

Sam: This food is stale.

Pam: How can you tell?

Sam: I cut my hand on the mashed potatoes!

Sam: Is that chili in your bowl?
Morty: Chilly? It's frozen solid!

Harve: Why did you bring your dad to school and make him sit on top of the kitchen freezer?

Marv: I wanted an ice-cold pop.

Veronica: Did you know the sandwich is named after the Earl of Sandwich?

Bill: How come?

Veronica: He was a member of the upper crust!

Mitch: Why are you serving raisins for dessert?

Cook: Those aren't raisins. They're very worried grapes!

Q: Can you define *bacteria*?

A: The rear entrance to the cafeteria!

Mary: Why are you eating your napkin?

Larry: Napkin?? So *that's* why it tasted so much better than everything else!

Mark: Who's the cook in this cafeteria?

Gary: It's a man with one eye called Bernie.

Mark: What's the other eye called?

Sam: What are you doing up here on the roof?

Mary: I heard today's lunch was on the house!

Pam: Why are you sitting here in the cafeteria, with a banana in your ear?

Sam: You'll have to speak louder. I have a banana in my ear!

Pam: Isn't that joke too old to go in this book?

Sam: What?

First Cafeteria Worker: Why were you late for work today?

Second Worker: I sprained my ankle.

First Worker: That's a lame excuse!

First Cafeteria Worker: Why were you late for work today?

Second Worker: I was hurrying till I got to that new sign outside the playground.

First Worker: What new sign?

Second Worker: The one that says, "School — go slow!"

First Cafeteria Worker: Why were you late for work today?

Second Worker: I was dreaming about a football game.

First Worker: So?

Second Worker: It went into overtime!

41

Boy on Phone: Mom, they're starving us here at boarding school.

Mother: Oh, dear. What are they feeding you?

Boy: Just breakfast, lunch, and dinner!

Q: What's worse than finding a worm in your apple?

A: Finding half a worm!

Teacher: Mickey, you didn't wipe your mouth after lunch, did you. I can see you had eggs for lunch.

Mickey: No, I didn't. I had pizza. I had eggs yesterday!

Mary: I hate cheese with holes.

Larry: Well, just eat the cheese and leave the holes on the side of your plate.

Will: Know why they call that huge thing a submarine sandwich?

Bill: No. Why?

Will: Because after eating it for a while, you have to come up for air!

Bill: That joke gave me a sinking feeling.

Pam: Why are you blowing so hard on your soup?

Sam: It's better than eating it!

Mary: Why aren't you eating your lunch?

Greg: I'm supposed to take these pills first. My doctor said to take two on an empty stomach.

Mary: Do they do any good?

Greg: I don't know. They keep rolling off my stomach every time I stand up!

Mary: Why are you jumping up and down like that?

Greg: I just took my medicine and forgot to shake the bottle!

Mary: Haven't you finished your alphabet soup yet?

Larry: No. I'm only up to the k's.

Ben: This bread is nice and warm.

Cook: It should be. My cat's been sitting on it all morning!

First Cafeteria Worker: You're late again. Why don't you get an alarm clock?

Second Worker: I did, but it keeps going off while I'm asleep!

Sam: Yesterday I was eating lunch, and that big kid over there threw pepper in my face.

Pam: That's terrible. What did you do?

Sam: Sneezed.

TOP 10
SCHOOL CAFETERIA DISHES
FOR THIS YEAR

10 THINGS THAT WILL HAPPEN TO YOU TODAY IN THE SCHOOL CAFETERIA

1. You won't realize your lunch tray is soaking wet until you've poured water down the front of your new sweater!

2. Someone will cut in front of you in line and say, "I was already here. You just didn't see me."

3. The kid ahead of you will take the last hamburger, and you'll be stuck with the squirrel rarebit.

4. You'll drop your loaded tray, and everyone will cheer and applaud.

5. Your fork will have green and yellow stuff stuck to it.

6. The kid who never closes his mouth when he chews will sit down right across from you.

7. Someone will make you laugh just as you start to drink your milk.

8. You will have a big green piece of spinach stuck to your front tooth, and no one will tell you.

9. You'll wonder how they make the Jell-O so tough to chew.

10. You'll promise yourself that you'll bring a bag lunch tomorrow!

WHAT'S COOKING?
THESE LUNCH LINE LAUGHS!

Robert: May I have a hamburger without mustard?

Cook: We're all out of mustard. But I can give it to you without ketchup!

Cook: You want a part-time job working in the cafeteria? Well, we need someone who is responsible.

Sam: That's me. On my last job, whenever anything went wrong, they said I was responsible!

Sharon: The food in this cafeteria tastes terrible!

Cafeteria Worker: I'm sorry you don't like it. Any other complaints?

Sharon: Yes. The portions are too small!

Q: Why does the cafeteria cook wear a white cap on her head?

A: Where else can she wear it?

Q: How do you make meat loaf?
A: Send it on vacation.

Q: How do you make a hamburger roll?

A: Give it a shove off a steep hill!

Q: What's green and flies a UFO?

A: A Martian who's just had lunch in a school cafeteria!

Q: What's white on the outside, green on the inside, and jumps?

A: A frog sandwich.

Q: Where is the best place to eat a hamburger?

A: In your mouth.

Bill: Aren't you eating lunch today?

Fred: No. I'm putting on too much weight.

Bill: What makes you say that?

Fred: At home, my mom had to let out the shower curtain!

Fred: You should eat more. You need to put on weight.

Bill: I know. This morning I stood sideways, and the teacher marked me absent!

Jerry: They aren't going to grow bananas any longer.

Mary: Really? Why not?

Jerry: They're already long enough!

Q: What's green and very dangerous?
A: Shark-infested lime Jell-O!

Q: What's yellow and fuzzy and goes up and down?

A: A peach in an elevator!

Sharon: Hey — your thumb is in my soup.

Cook: That's okay. The soup's not hot.

Fred: There's a fly swimming in my soup.

Cook: What do you expect me to do — call a lifeguard?!

Bill: There's no chicken in this chicken soup.

Cook: So what? You don't get any dog in a dog biscuit, do you!

Sally: Hey — my plate's wet.

Cook: That's not wet. That's the soup!

Sam: There's a dead fly in my soup.
Cook: Well, we can't always
   guarantee you'll get a live one!

Bill: There's a dead ant in my soup.
Cook: Yes. They're not very good
   swimmers.

Q: How do you say school cafeteria in French?

A: School cafeteria in French.

Stuart: How old is this meat loaf?

Cafeteria Worker: I don't know. I've only worked here a month!

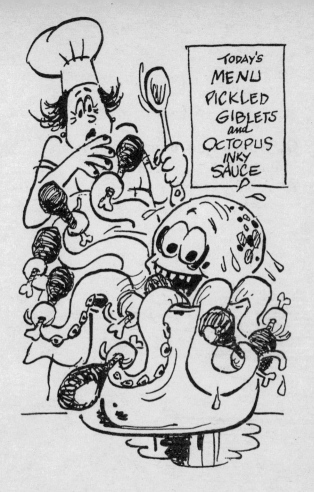

Q: What did the cafeteria cook get when he crossed a chicken with an octopus?

A: Drumsticks for everybody!

Q: What's long, orange, and wears diapers?

A: A baby carrot.

Q: What's purple and goes "putt putt putt"?

A: An outboard grape.

Q: What's black and white and green every afternoon?

A: A zebra that eats in the school cafeteria!

Marty: Do you serve shrimps in this cafeteria?

Cook: Take a tray. We'll serve anyone.

Q: Why did the lobster blush?

A: He saw the salad dressing.

Q: What's the monster's favorite cafeteria food?

A: Grave-y.

First Cafeteria Worker: We're serving a thousand things to eat today.
Second Worker: Really? What?
First Worker: Beans!

MORE FOOD FOOLISHNESS

Ted: Why do you have blocks in your lunch bag?

Fred: My doctor said I should have three square meals a day!

Ed: Why do you have bandages in your lunch bag?

Ned: For the cold cuts!

Fred: Why do you have a flashlight in your lunch box?

Ted: My mom said to eat a light lunch!

Ollie: Why do you have a toy train in your lunch bag?

Molly: My mom said I should choo-choo my food!

Q: Do you know how to make ground beef chili?

A: Put it in the freezer!

Pam: Aren't you going to the cafeteria today?

Sam: No. It's a complete waste of time.

Pam: What do you mean?

Sam: Well, five hours after I eat there, I'm hungry again!

Q: What did the boy in the cafeteria get when he spilled his bowl of chicken soup!

A: Wet!

Sally: Is the chicken fresh?
Cook: You bet. I had to slap her face this morning!

Sally: Why is the chicken soup green?
Cook: That's odd. It wasn't green when I made it three weeks ago.

Q: How do you make a tuna melt?
A: Put him in a very hot room.

Jerry: Do you know how to make an elephant sandwich?

Mary: No. How?

Jerry: First, get two very large pieces of bread. . . .

Dave: I wasn't paying attention and I accidentally swallowed my teaspoon.

Susan: Don't stir.

Dave: I wasn't paying attention and just swallowed a roll of film.

Susan: I hope nothing develops.

Dave: I wasn't paying attention and just swallowed a pencil. What should I do?

Susan: Use a pen.

Dave: I wasn't paying attention and just swallowed my lunch.

Susan: Ha ha. That's the funniest joke yet!